PAINTINGS FROM SOMEWHERE ELSE

AN EXHIBITION BY

CHRIS STEVENS AND NICK RANDS

Chris Stevens is based in Caunes Minervois, France and London, UK. He studied Fine Art at the University of Reading and has exhibited regularly since graduating in 1978.

Solo exhibitions include: Beaux Arts, London; PM Gallery, London; Smelik & Stokking and Galerie Rademakersin Amsterdam, GlynnVivian Museum & Art Gallery, Swansea and Howard Gardens Gallery, Cardiff.
Group shows include: REALITY, Sainsbury Centre and The Walker Art Gallery,UK; Fussball in Der Kunst, Germany; BP Portrait Award, National Portrait Gallery, London and Heads, Flowers East, London. Public collections include the Victoria & Albert Museum, The National Gallery of Wales, Unilever, Galerija Portreta, Bosnia & Hertzegovena and many private collections in the UK, South Africa, USA and Europe.

www.chrisstevens.co

Nick Rands is based in Caunes Minervois, France and Porto Alegre, Brazil. He studied Fine Art at he University of Reading and Art Education at Bristol University. He has also worked as an art teacher, education-programme coordinator and translator. He was Southern Arts Brazil Exchange Artist in 1992 and has lived in Brazil since 1998.

Recent solo exhibitions include: Horizontes Terrestres, ESPM Porto Alegre (2017), Neckinger River Levels, Bermondsey Yard, London (2015), Um Quadrado no Rio Grande do Sul, Museu Julio de Castilhos, Porto Alegre (2012), A Gente, Museu do Trabalho, Porto Alegre (2011), ChromaLife, Brick house, London (2009). Group shows include: Magmart/video art festival, Casoria Contemporary Art Museum, Naples, Italy (2013), Digital Graffiti, Florida USA (2010, 2013, 2016), 7 Billionth Citizen Townhouse Gallery, Cairo, Solent Showcase, Southampton, UK and Mamute, Porto Alegre (2013), 8th Mercosul Biennial, Porto Alegre (2011).

www.nickrands.com

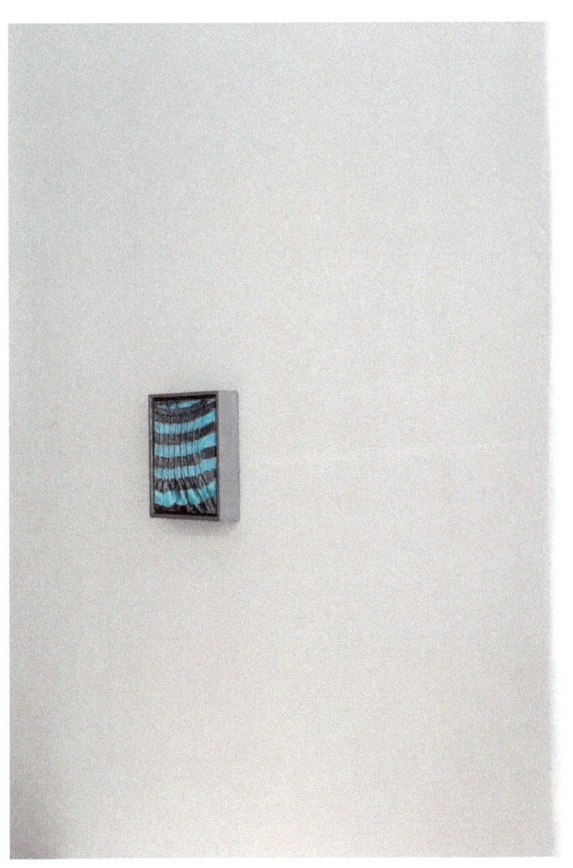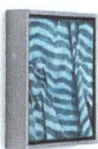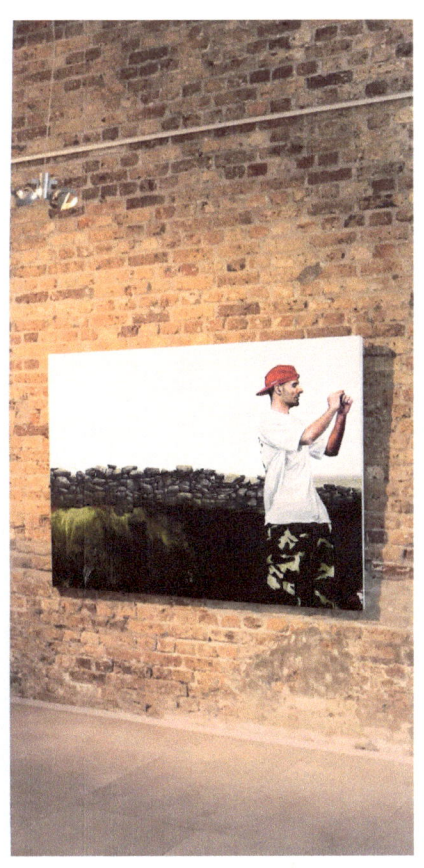

Youngblood Gallery, 70 - 72 Bree Street, Cape Town, South Africa

November 2017

Paintings from somewhere else. Chris Stevens | Nick Rands

The title hints at similarities and differences. The exhibition is of paintings, but they come from somewhere else, from different continents but also from different places within each artist. On the one hand from a world of the human figure, of the gesture and expression which communicate in a direct way aspects of the vitality of contemporary (urban?) life; on the other hand from an ephemeral world of fabrics, patterns and weaves, of garments worn, and wearing out. Grand gesture and intimate gaze. In both cases, painting might be said to lend more permanence and 'weight' to subject matter that may sometimes be considered marginal: ordinary people, commonplace objects are depicted in the time-consuming practice with a 600-year history, of painting in oil paint on canvas. That history itself – its great masters and lesser figures – has a strong influence on the work of each of these artists, in a practice of more than 40 years but in which both would admit they discover something new with each picture.

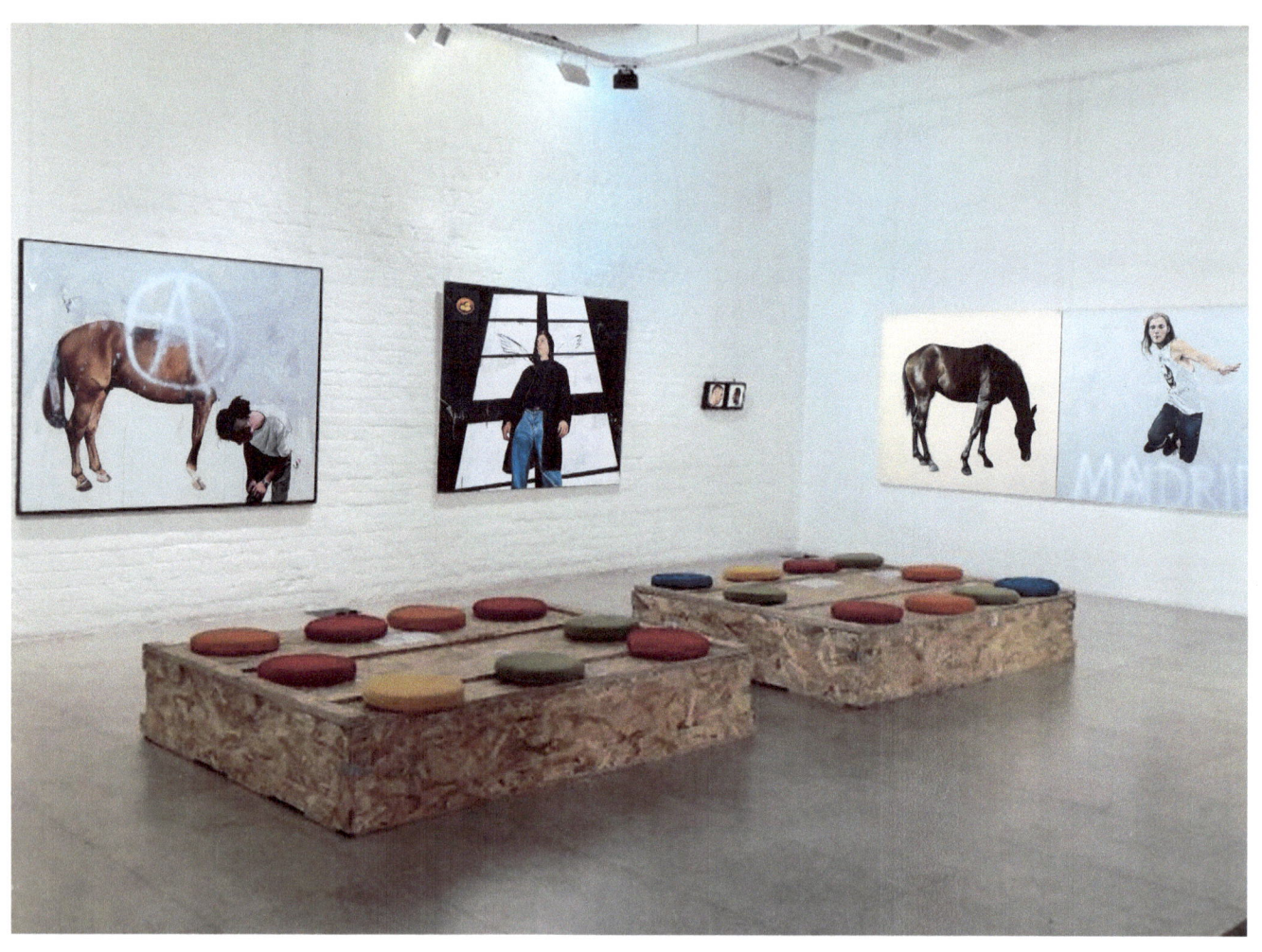

Chris Stevens

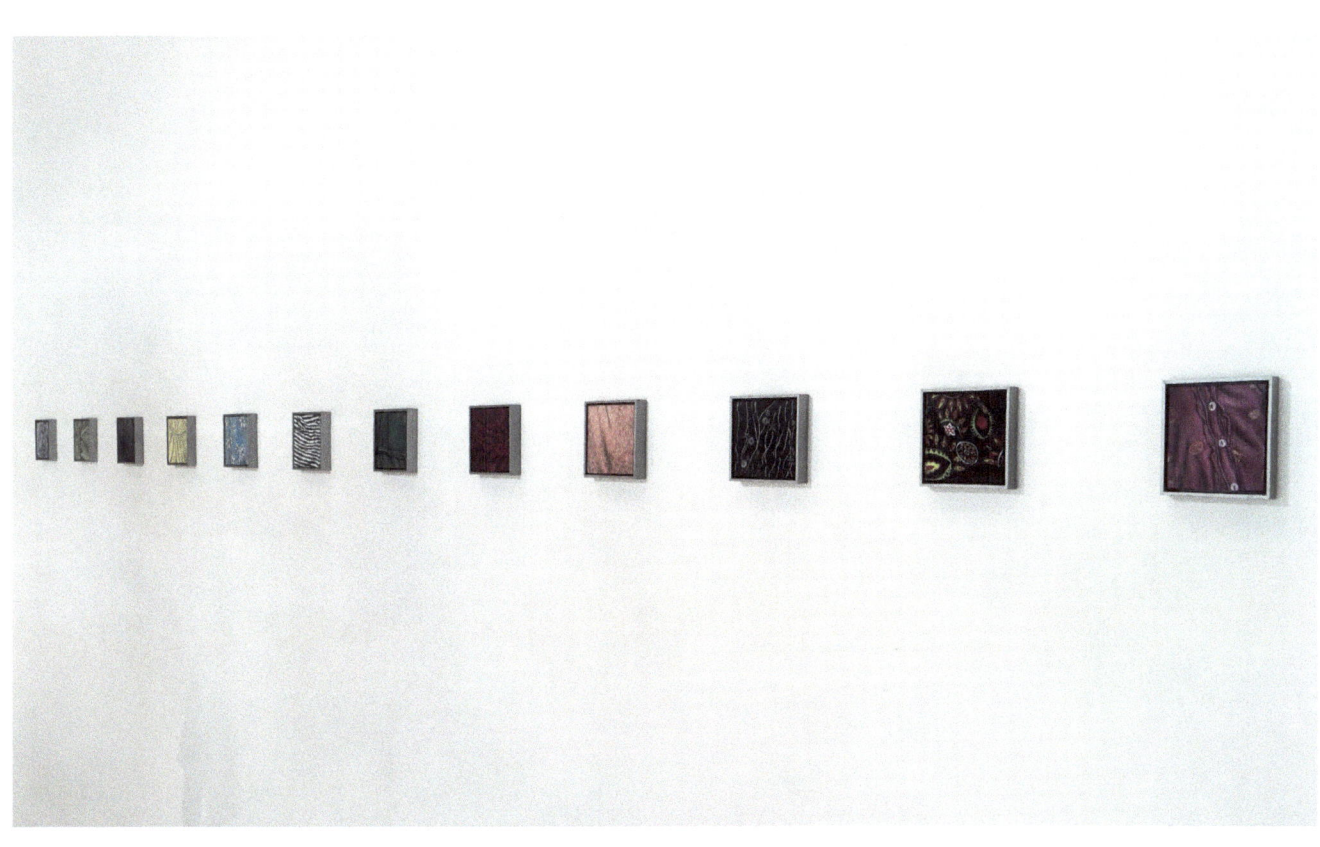

Nick Rands

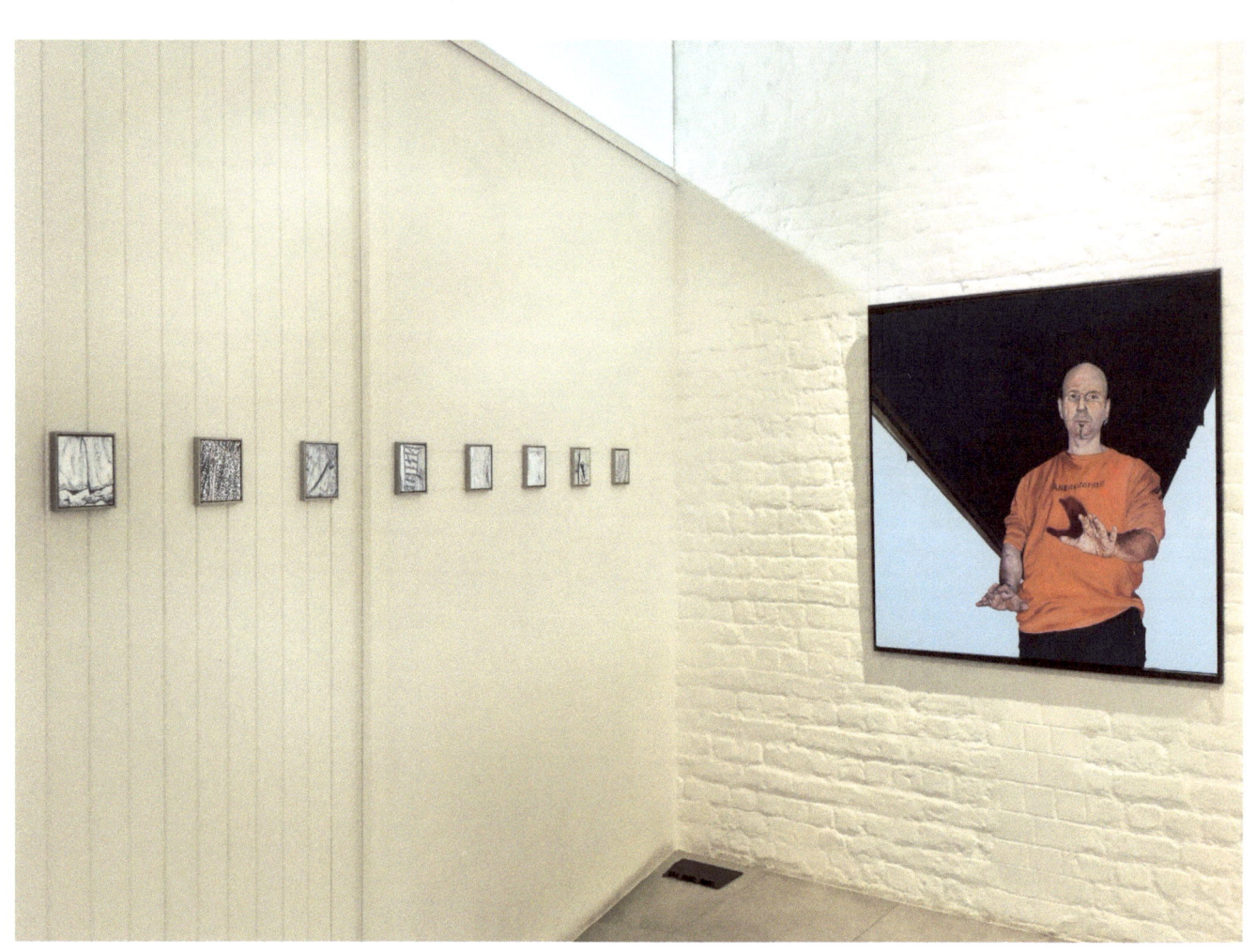

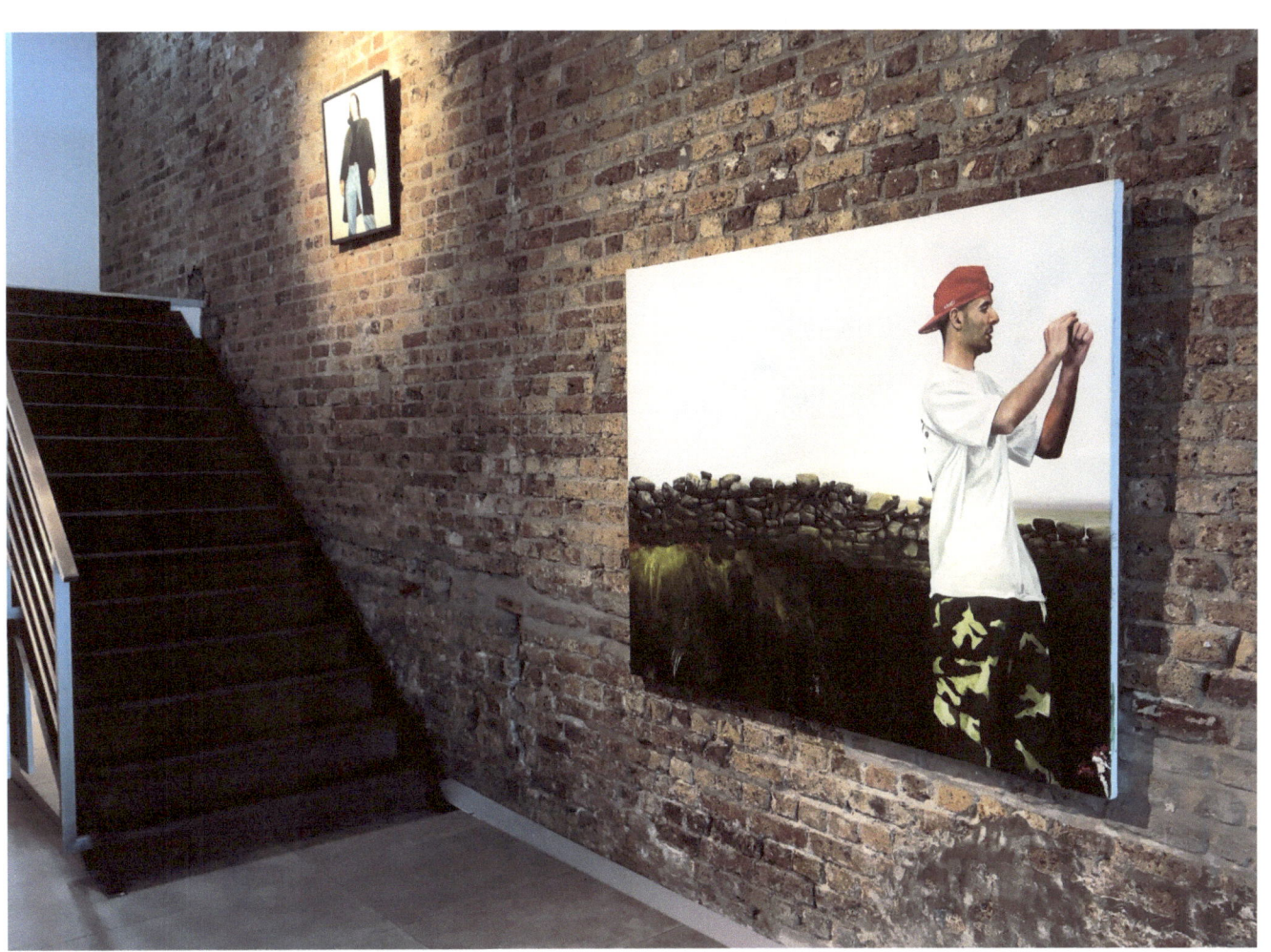

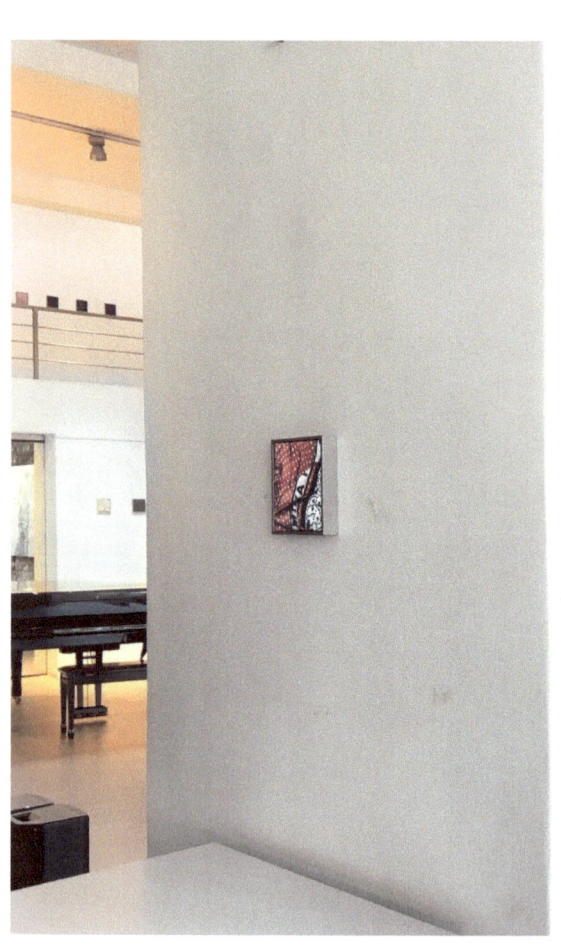
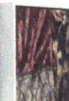
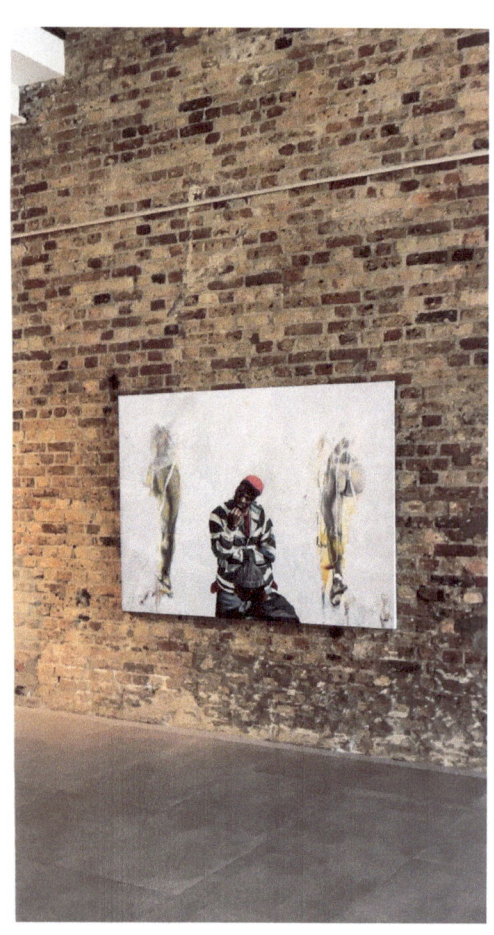

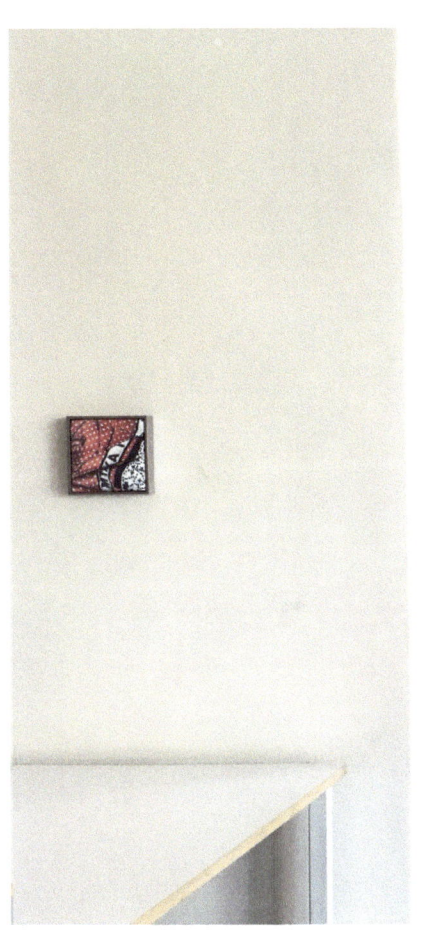
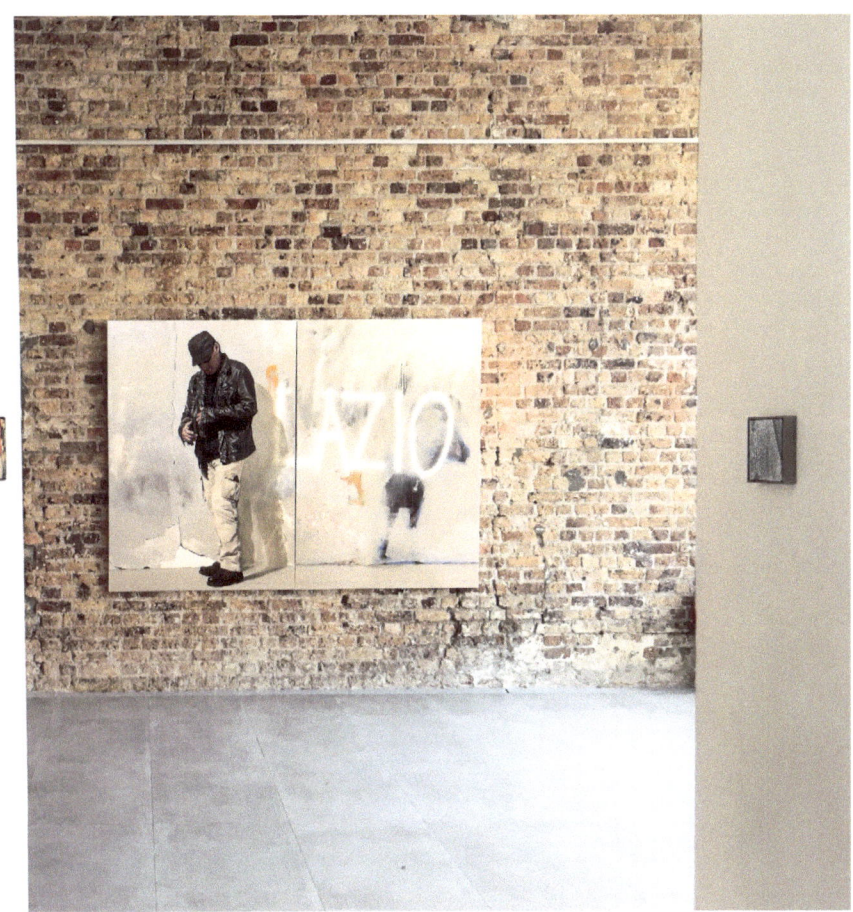

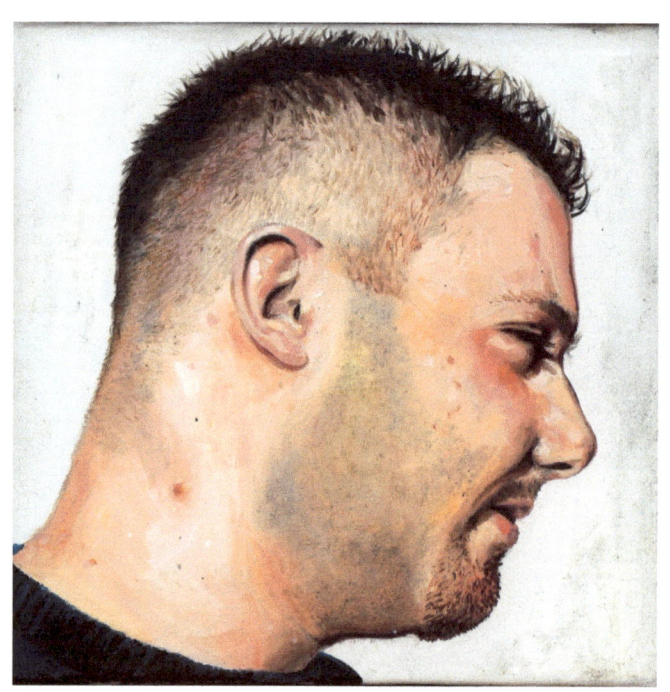

Chris Stevens
Ratty, 2010
Oil on canvas
20 x 20 cm

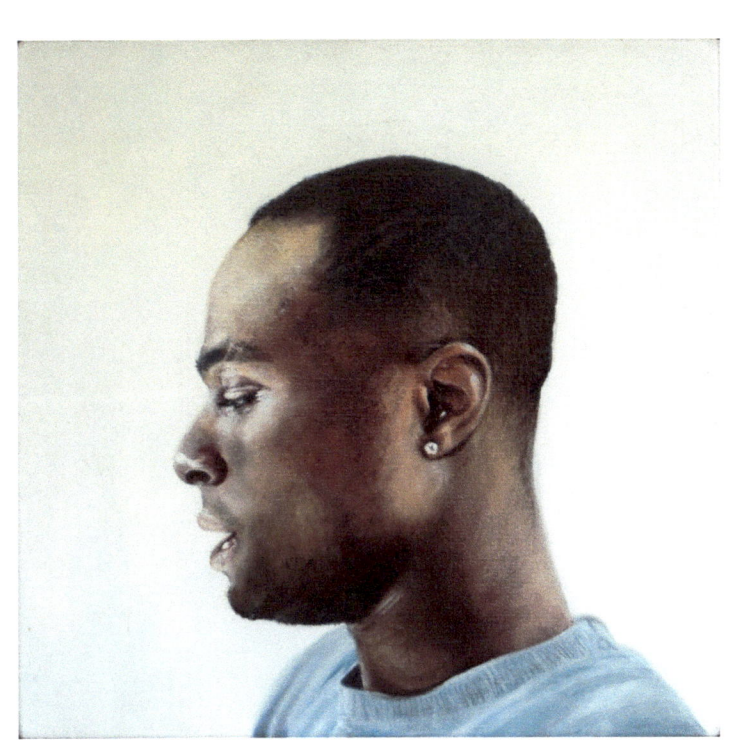

Chris Stevens
Josiah, 2017
Oil on canvas
20 x 20 cm

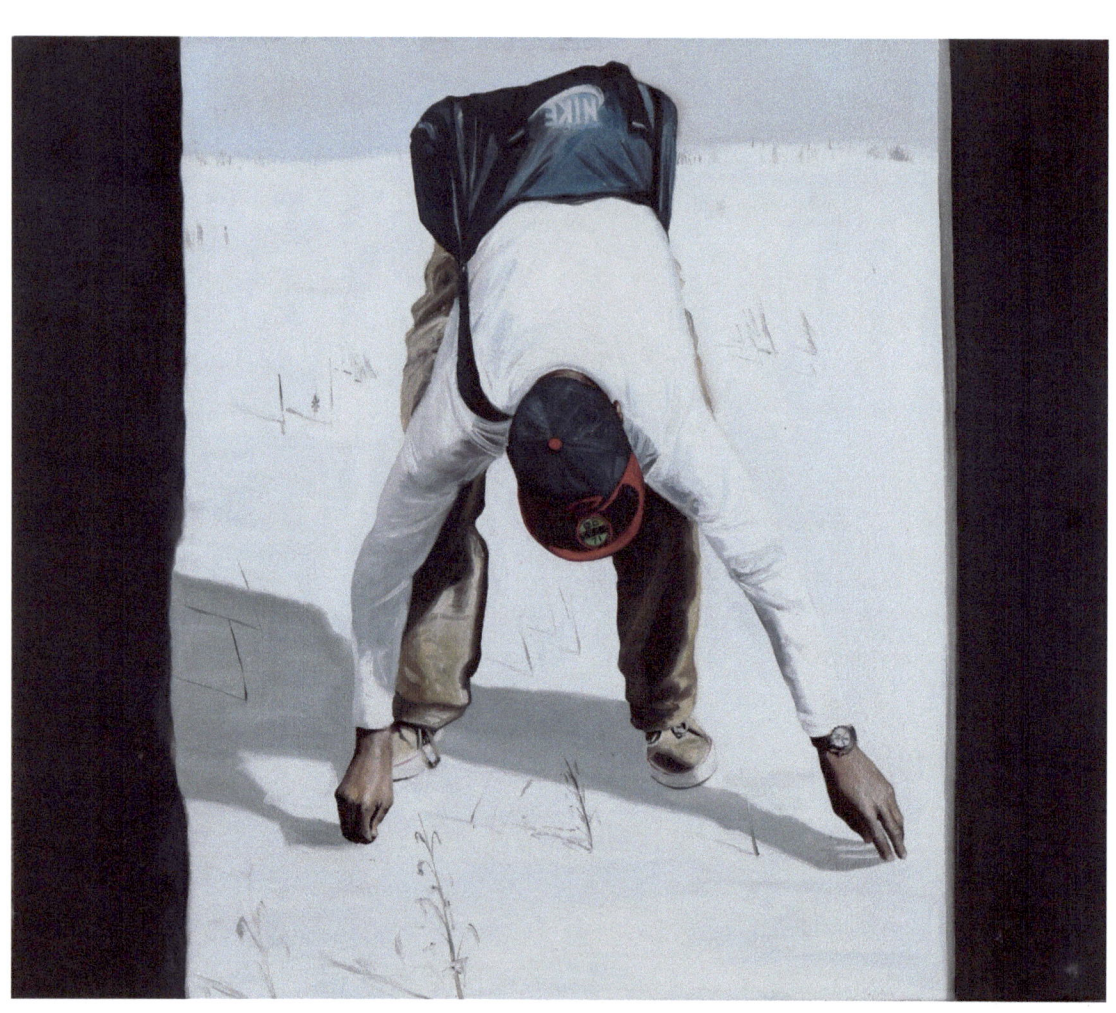

Chris Stevens
Homeland, 2012
Oil on canvas
102 x 122 cm

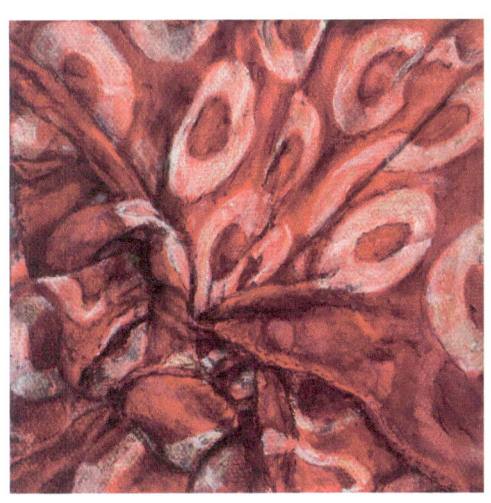

Nick Rands
Ausência series, 2015-17
Oil on Canvas
12 x 12 cm

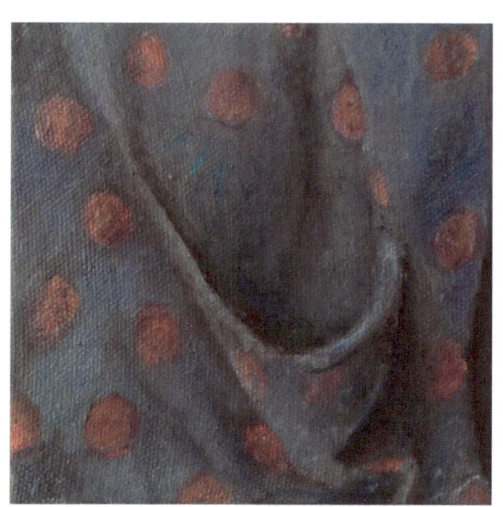

Nick Rands
Ausência series, 2015-17
Oil on Canvas
12 x 12 cm

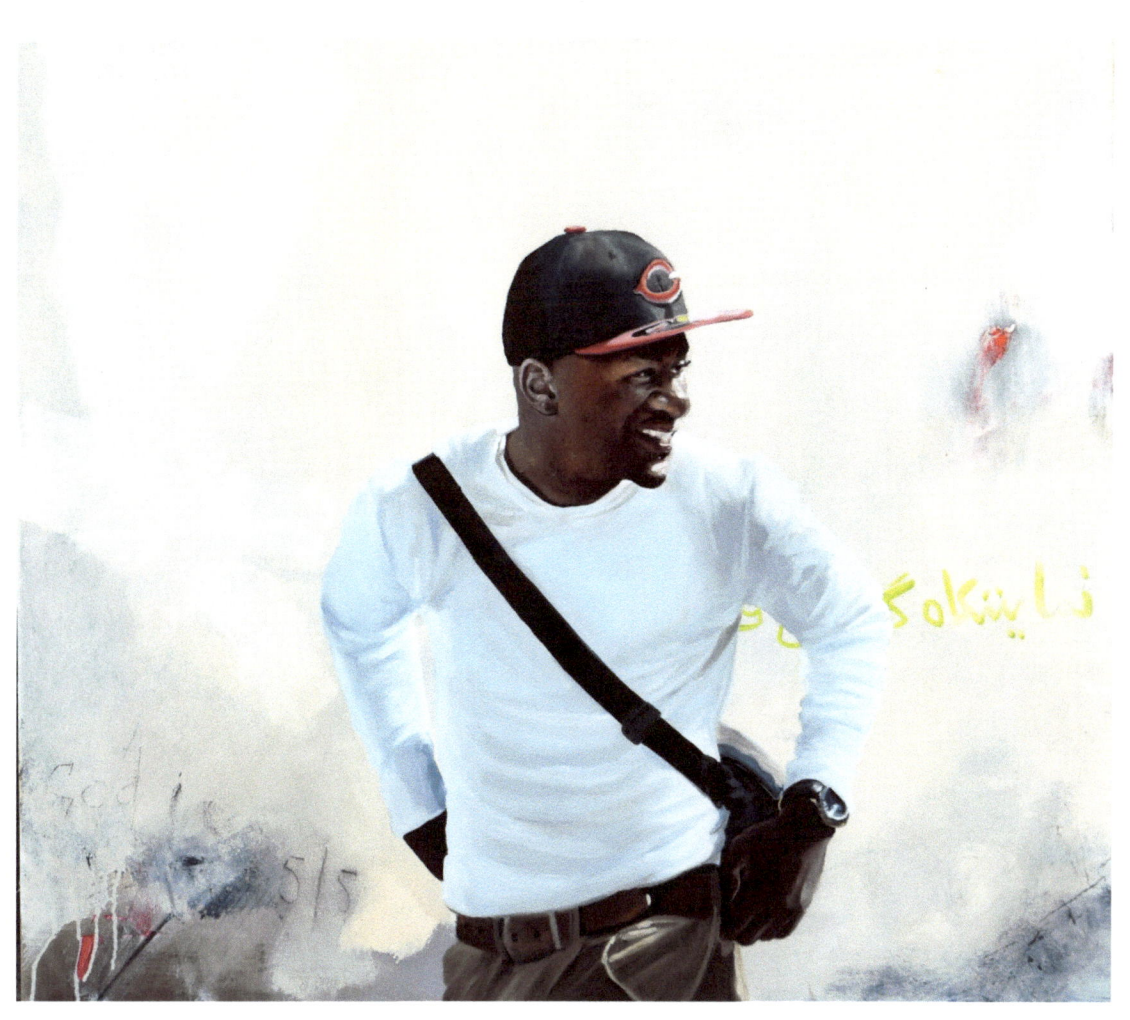

Chris Stevens
The Fifth day of May, 2016
Oil on canvas
80 x 90 cm

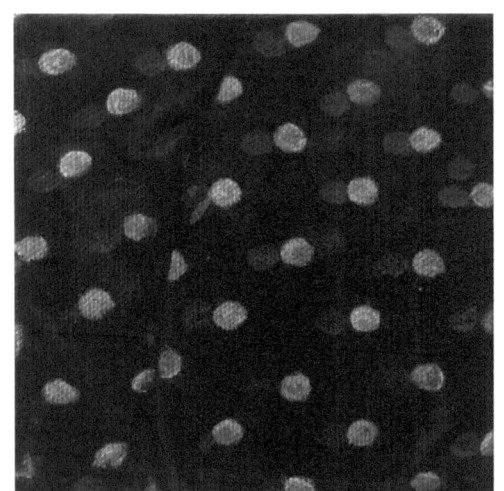
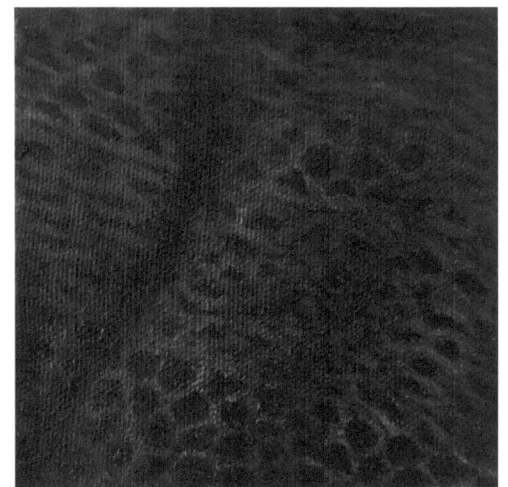

Nick Rands
Ausência series, 2015-17
Oil on Canvas
12 x 12 cm

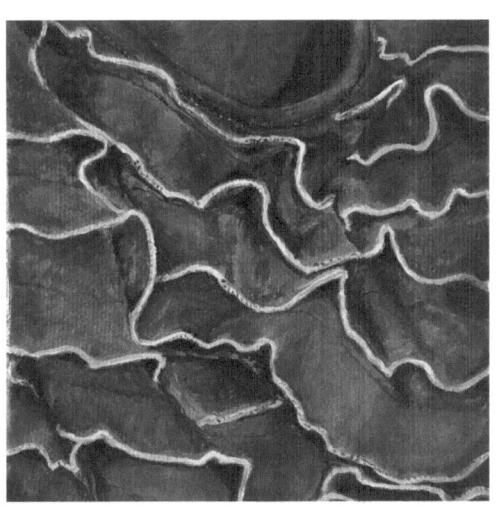 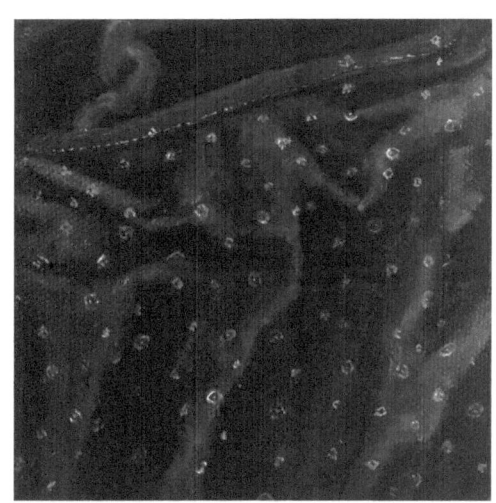

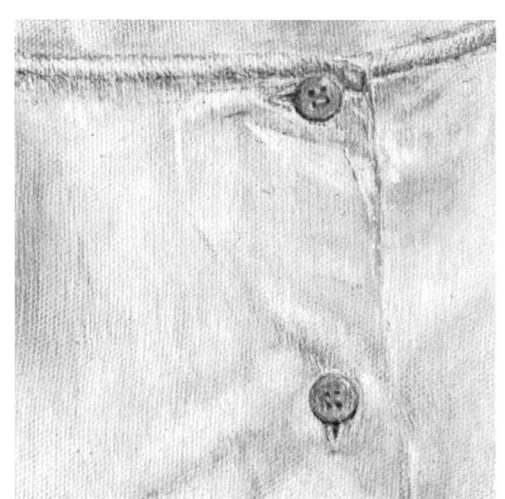 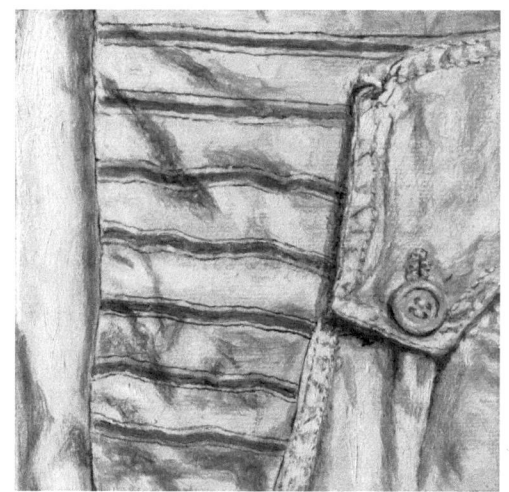

Nick Rands
Ausência series, 2015-17
Oil on Canvas
12 x 12 cm

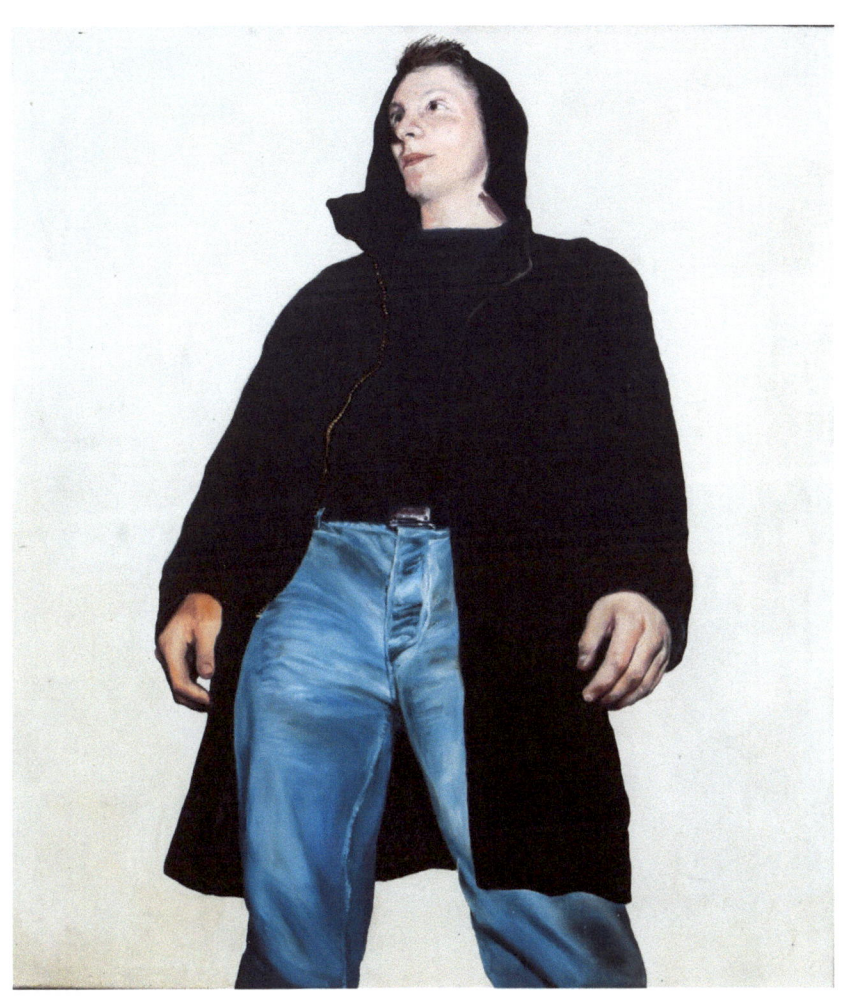

Chris Stevens
Soulful House, 2005
Oil on canvas
70 x 60 cm

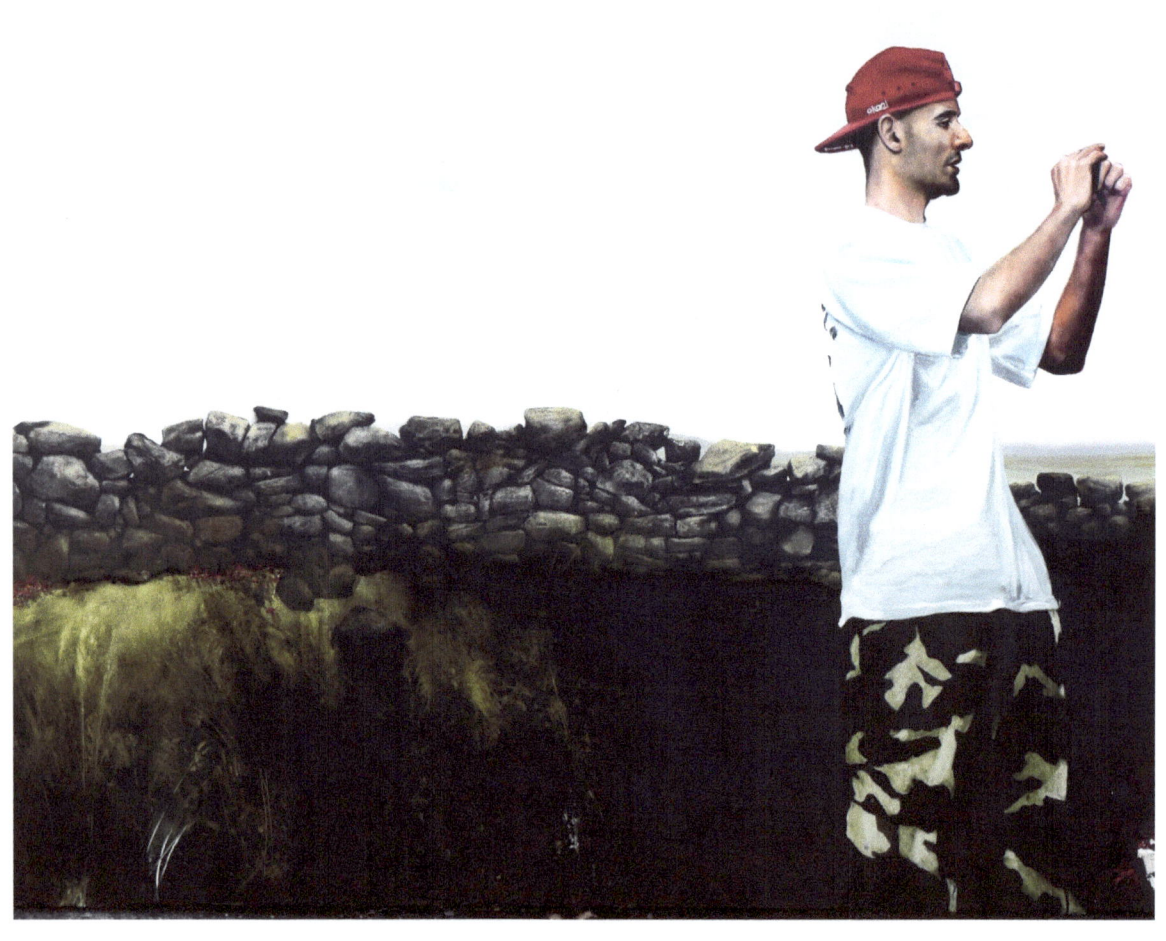

Chris Stevens
How to prove you exist, 2017
Oil on canvas
150 x 180 cm

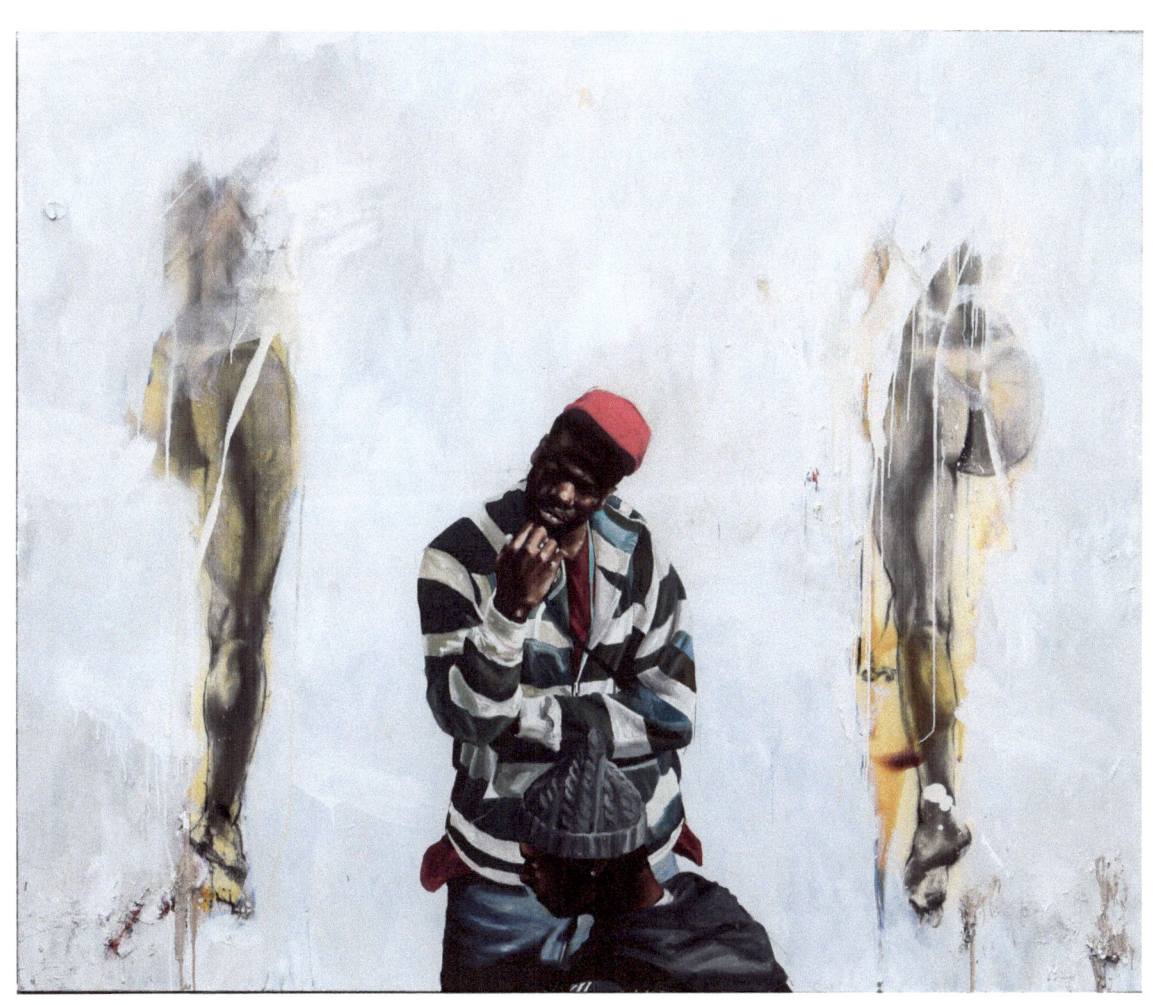

Chris Stevens
Panorama, 2007
Oil on canvas
150 x 180 cm

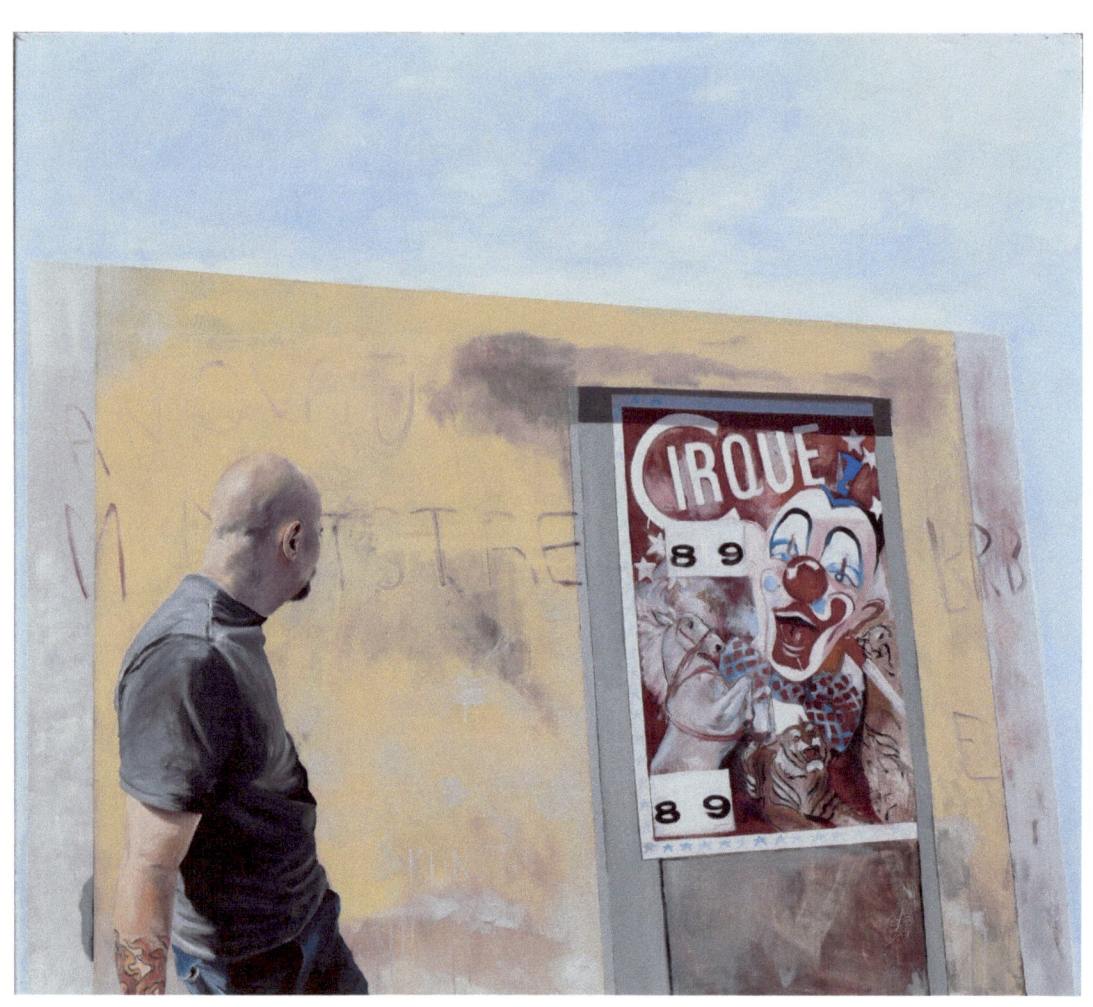

Chris Stevens
Steve goes to the Circus, 2010
Oil on canvas
120 x 150 cm

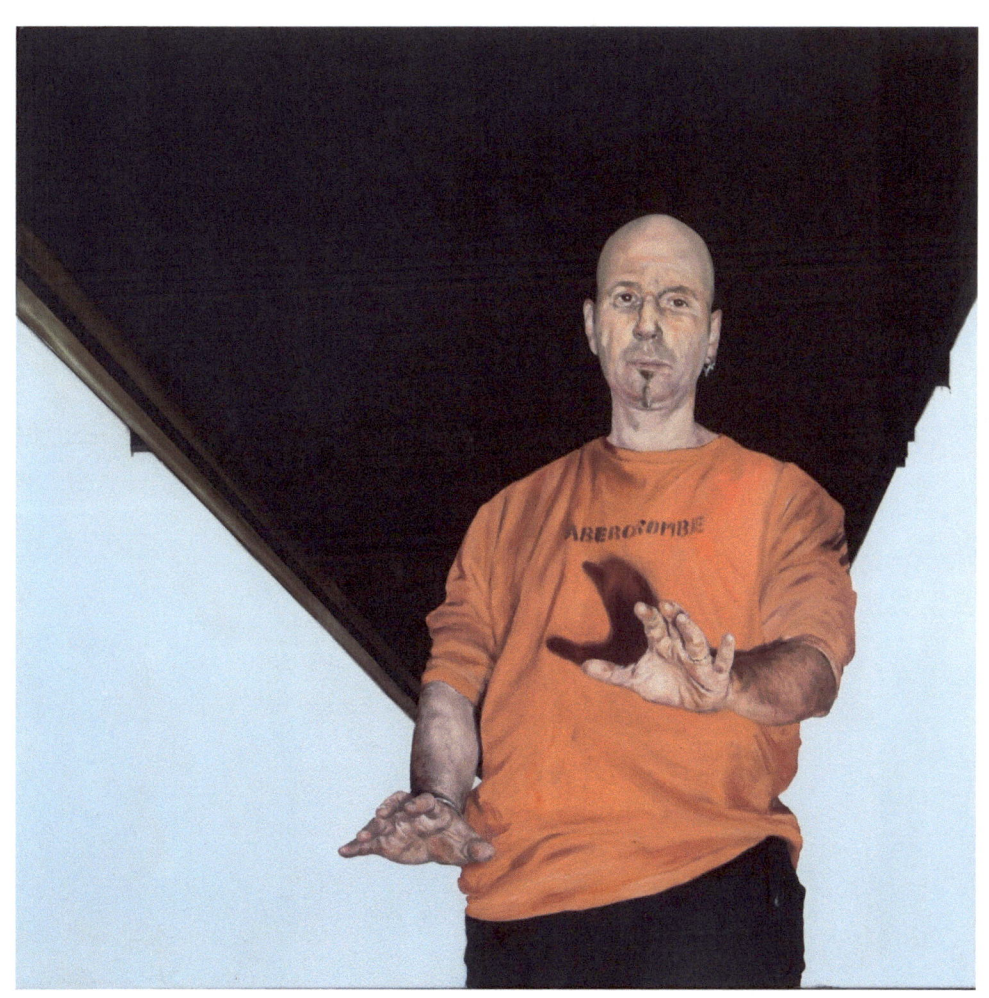

Chris Stevens
Flyover, 2008
Oil on canvas
120 x 120 cm

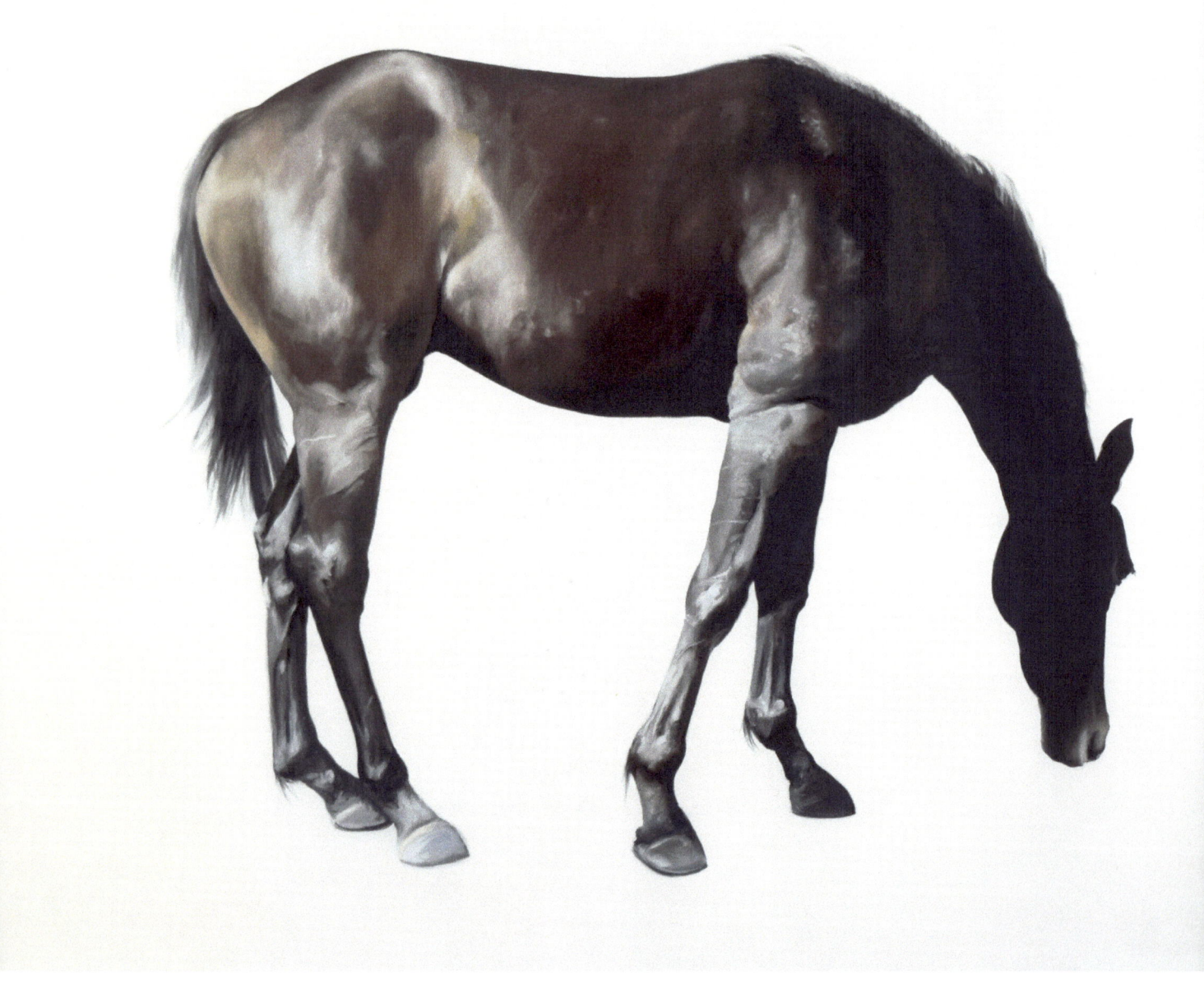

Chris Stevens
A Momentary Lapse in the Understanding of the effect of Gravity, 2017
Oil on canvas
150 x 340 cm

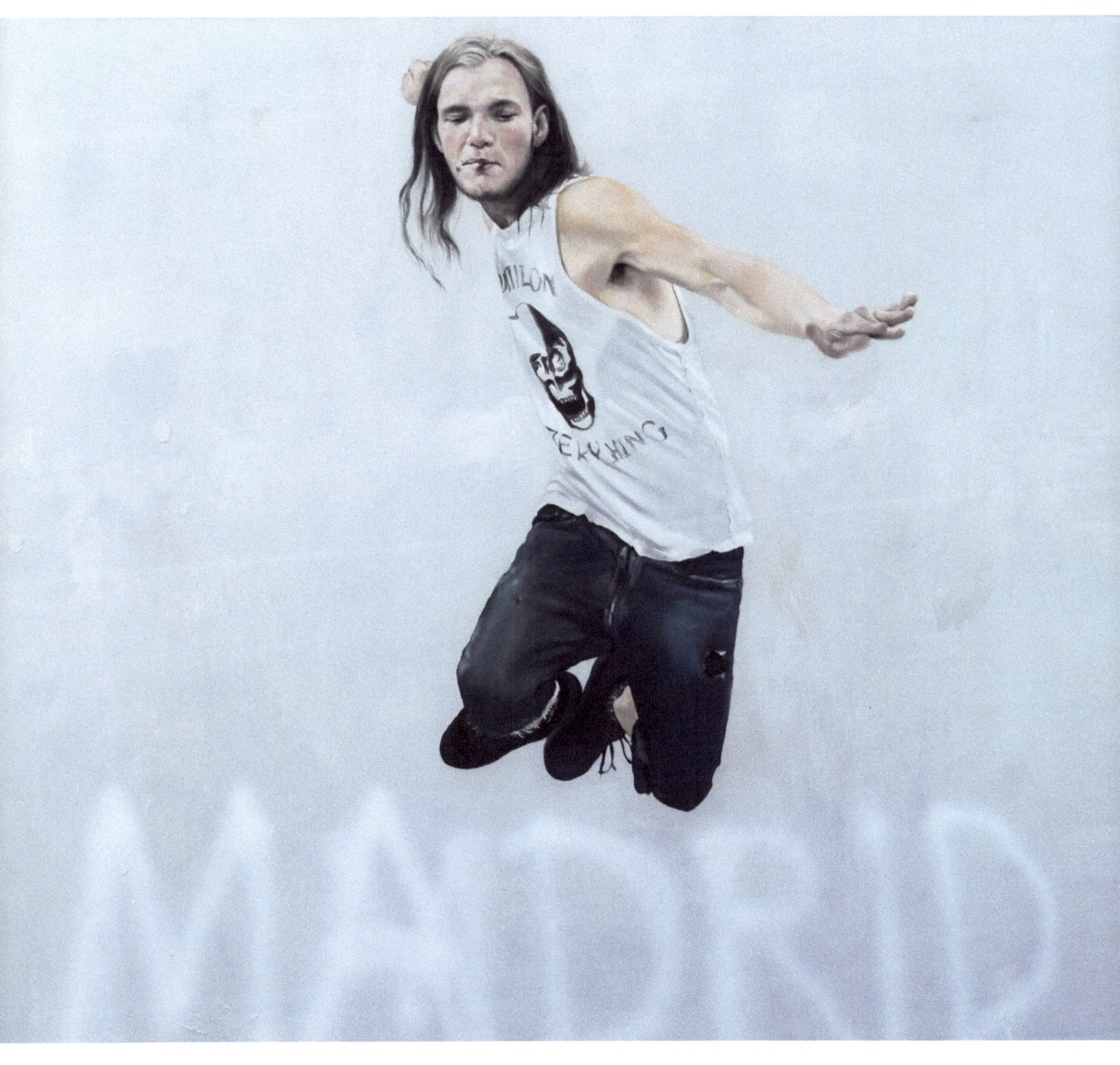

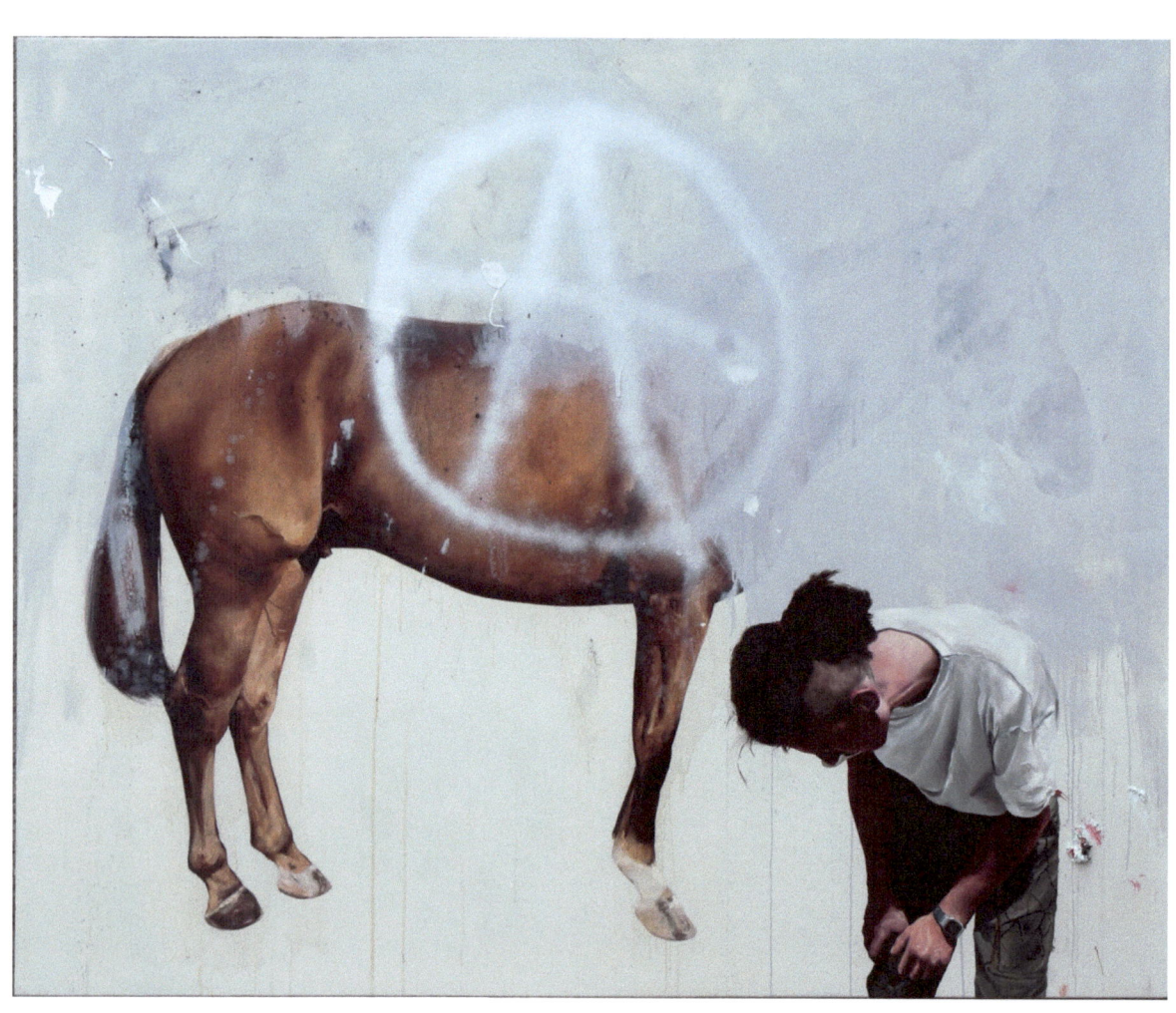

Chris Stevens
La Peau des Murs, 2015
Oil on canvas
180 x 150 cm

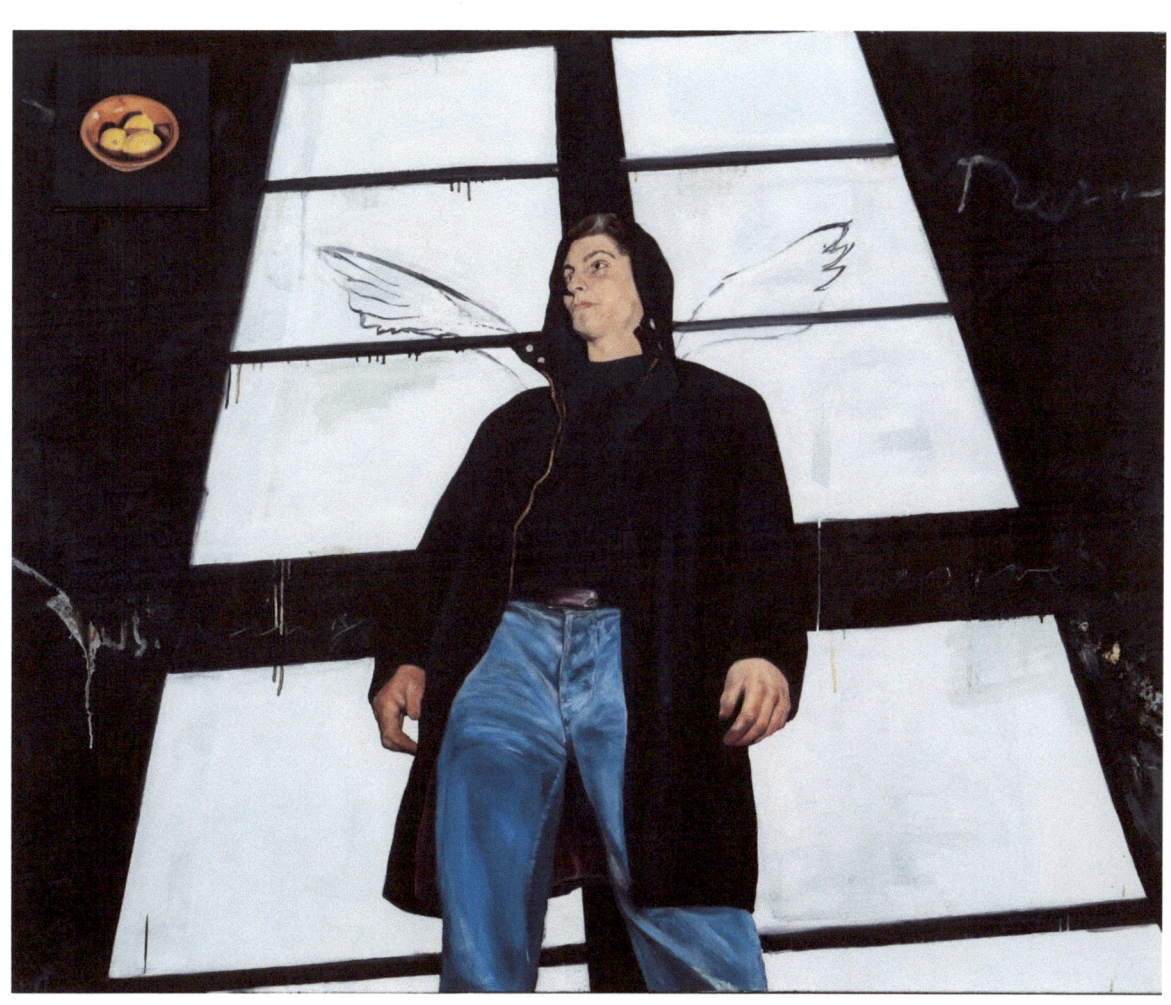

Chris Stevens
Lemon, 2006
Oil on canvas
150 x 180 cm

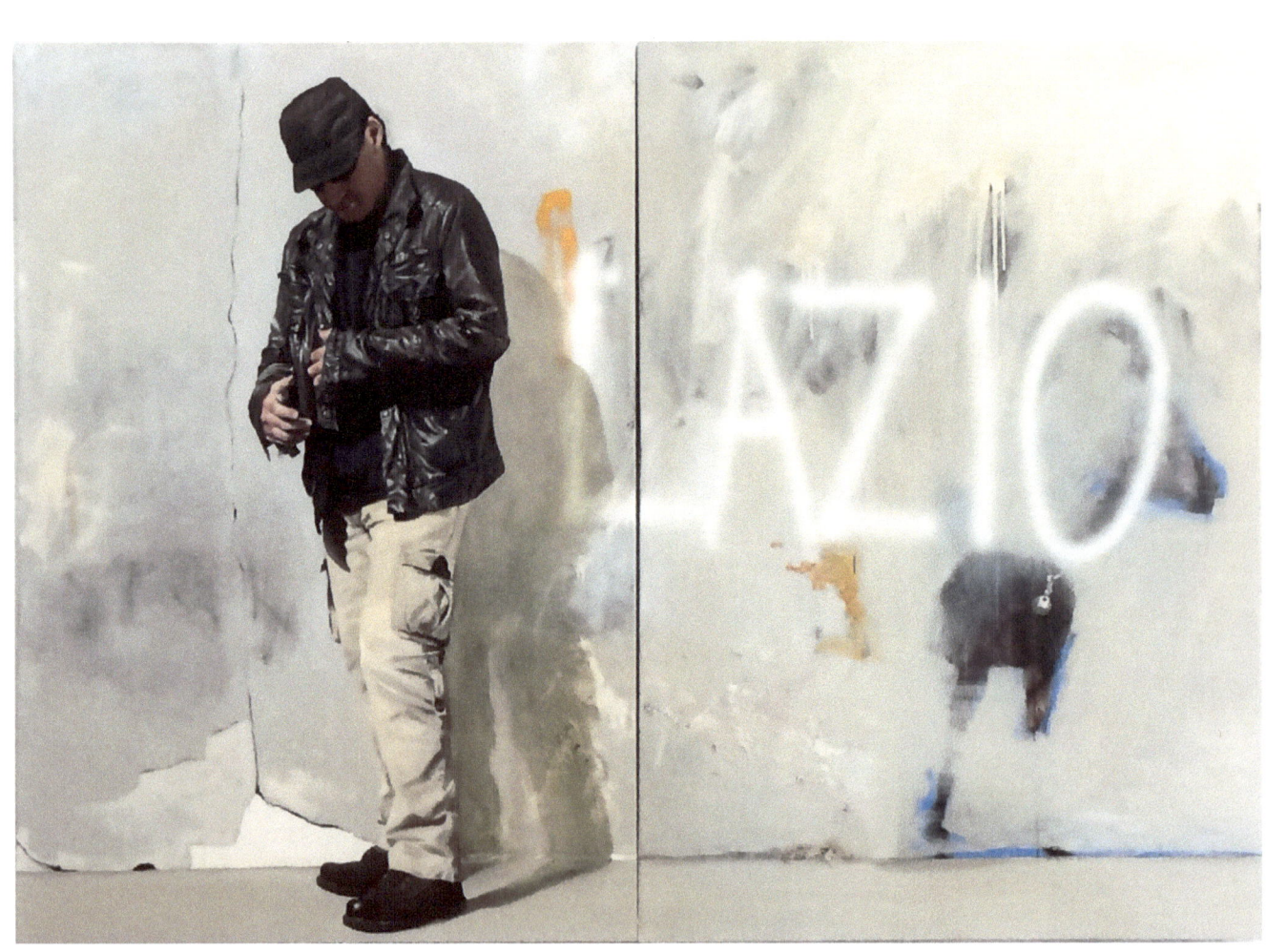

Chris Stevens
Lazio stole Gazza, 2016
Oil on canvas
175 x 240 cm

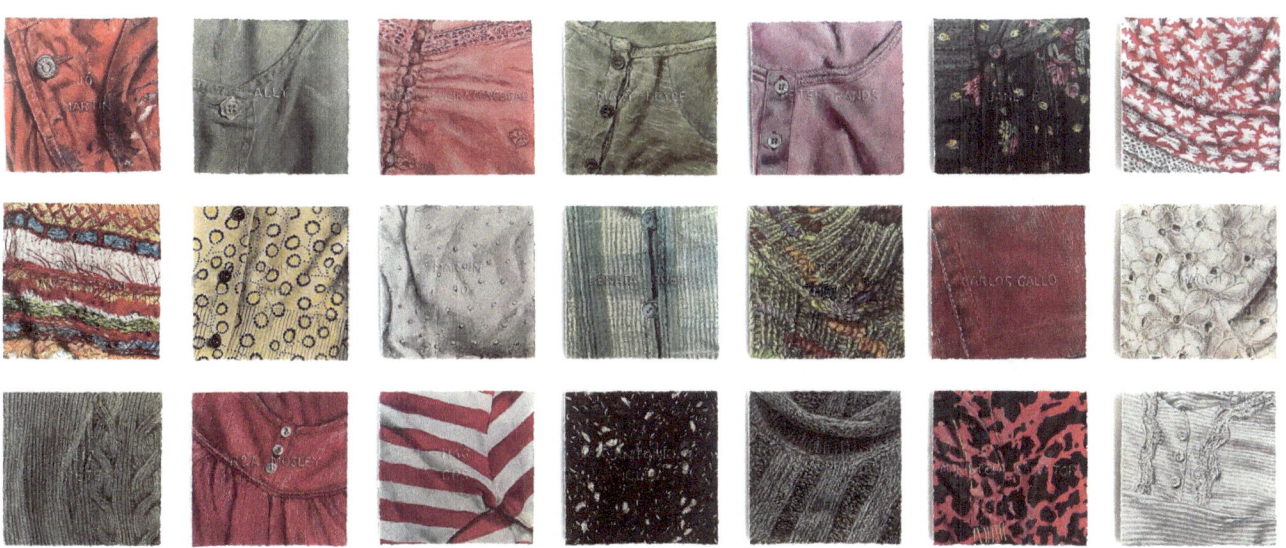

Nick Rands
Guardians of absence series, 2017
Giclée print with embossing on Hahnemühle photo rag paper
12 x 12 cm

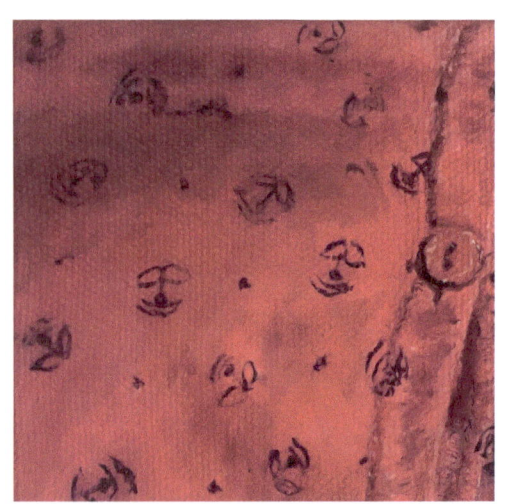 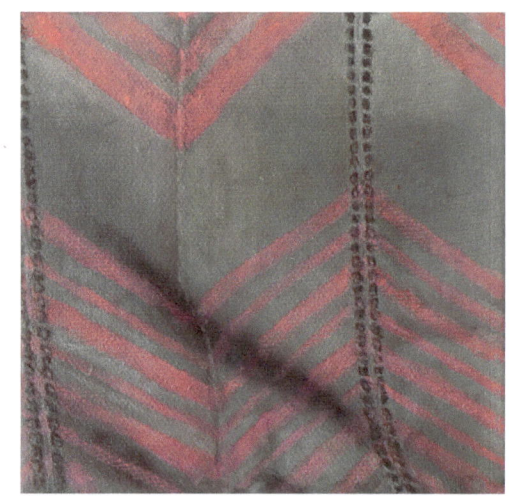

Nick Rands
Ausência series, 2015-17
Oil on Canvas
12 x 12 cm

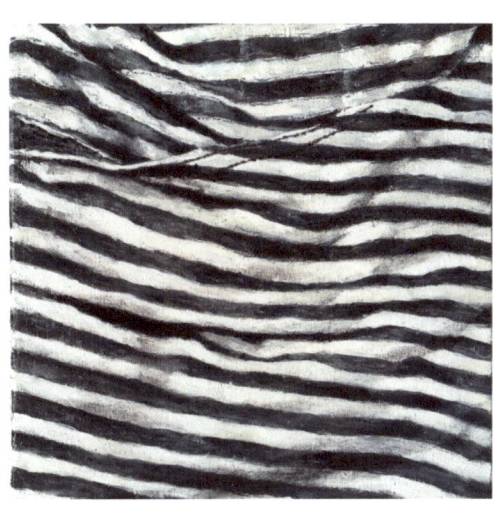 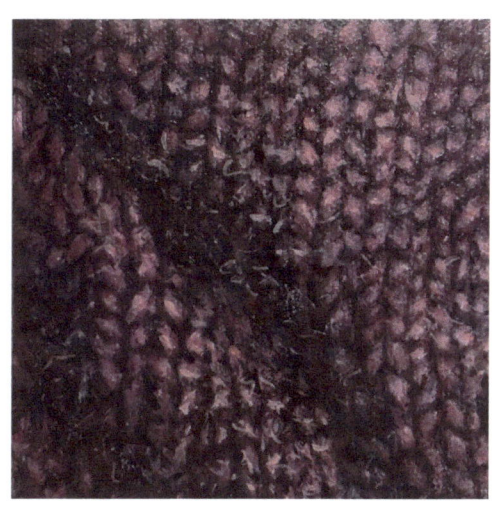

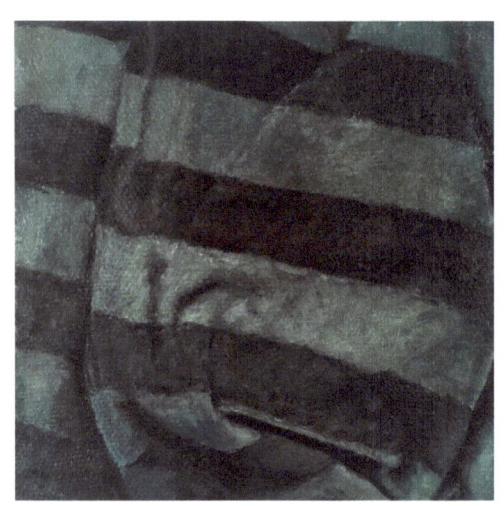
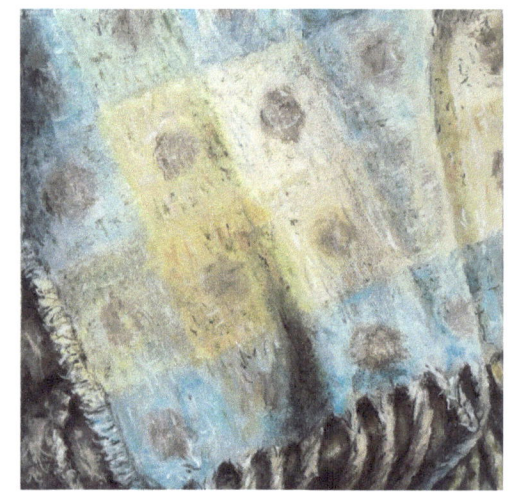

Nick Rands
Ausência series, 2015-17
Oil on Canvas
12 x 12 cm

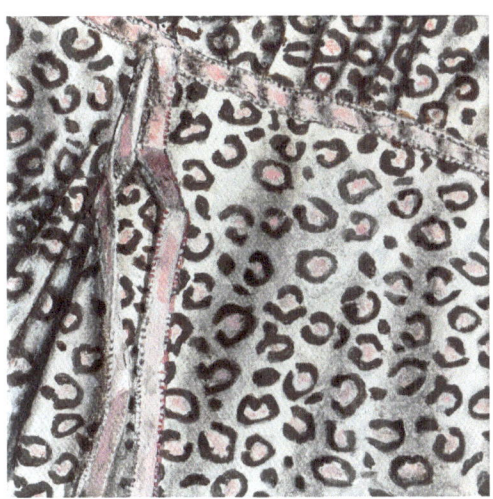
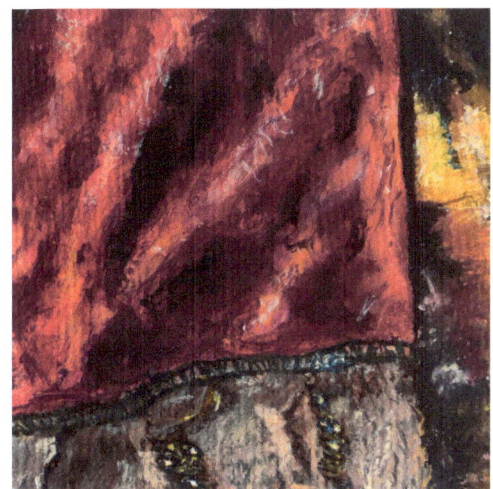

Thanks to:
Steve Harley, Marie Voghts, Ina Wichterich, Natasha Fortuin, Wonga Bushe

www.ingramcontent.com/pod-product-compliance
Lightning Source LLC
Chambersburg PA
CBHW051819210526
45473CB00005B/1667